The Progress of Insight

(Visuddhi-ñāṇa-kathā)

A Modern Pali Treatise on
Buddhist Satipaṭṭhāna Meditation

The Venerable
Mahāsi Sayādaw

Translated from the Pali with Notes by
Nyānaponika Thera

BUDDHIST   PUBLICATION   SOCIETY
KANDY   ·   SRI LANKA

Buddhist Publication Society
P.O. Box 61
54, Sangharaja Mawatha
Kandy, Sri Lanka
http://www.bps.lk

First edition published in 1965.
Reprinted 1978, 1985, 1994, 2006, 2014

National Library and Documentation Service Board -
Cataloguing-in-Publication Data

Mahāsi Sayādaw himi

The Progress of Insight: a modern pali treatise on Buddhist
Satipaṭṭhāna meditation / Mahāsi Sayādaw himi.- reprint.-
Kandy: Buddhist Publication Society, 2014

BP504.- 64p.; 12.5cm

ISBN 978-955-24-0089-9

i. 294.34435 DDC23   ii. Title

1. Meditation, Buddhism

Typeset at the BPS
Text set in Times_BPS, headings in Helvetica_BPS

Printed by,
Samayawardana Printers
Colombo 10.

Ven. Mahāsi Sayādaw

CONTENTS

TRANSLATOR'S FOREWORD

To present to the reading public a treatise on Buddhist meditation needs no word of apology today. In wide circles of the West, Buddhist meditation is no longer regarded as a matter of purely academic or exotic interest. Under the stress and complexity of modern life the need for mental and spiritual regeneration is now widely felt, and in the field of the mind's methodical development the value of Buddhist meditation has been recognised and tested by many.

It is, in particular, the Buddha's Way of Mindfulness *(satipaṭṭhāna)* that has been found invaluable because it is adaptable to, and beneficial in, widely different conditions of life. The present treatise is based on this method of cultivating mindfulness and awareness, which ultimately aims at the mind's final liberation from greed, hatred, and delusion.

The author of this treatise, the Venerable Mahāsi Sayādaw (U Sobhana Mahāthera), is a Buddhist monk of contemporary Burma and an eminent meditation master. A brief sketch of his life is included in this volume. The path of meditation described in these pages was, and still is, taught by him in his meditation centre called Thathana Yeiktha, in Rangoon, and is also set forth in his lectures and books in the Burmese language.

The framework of the treatise is provided by the classical "seven stages of purification" *(satta-visuddhi)*, just as in Acariya Buddhaghosa's famous *Visuddhimagga*. On gradually reaching these stages, various phases of insight knowledge *(ñāṇa)* are developed, leading on to the stages of ultimate liberation. The approach followed is that of "bare insight" *(sukkha-vipassanā)* where, by direct observation, one's own bodily and mental processes are seen with increasing clarity as being impermanent, liable to suffering, and without a self or soul. The meditational practice begins with a few selected subjects of body-contemplation, which are retained up to the very end of the road. With the gradually increasing strength of mindfulness and concentration the range widens and the vision deepens until the insight knowledges unfold themselves in due order, as a natural outcome of the practice. This approach to the ultimate goal of Buddhist meditation is called *bare insight* because insight into the three characteristics of existence is made use of exclusively here, dispensing with the prior development of full concentrative absorption *(jhāna)*. Nevertheless, and it hardly needs mention, here too a high degree of mental concentration is required for perseverance in the practice, for attaining to insight knowledge, and for reaping its fruits.

As stated in the treatise itself (p. 5), it is not the author's purpose to give a detailed introduction to the practice for the use of beginners. The foremost concern in this work is with a stage where, after diligent preliminary practice, the insight knowledges have begun to emerge, leading up to the highest crest of spiritual achievement, arahantship. Of the basic exercises, the treatise gives only a brief indication, at the beginning of Chapter I. Detailed instruction about these may be gathered by the student from the author's *Practical Insight Meditation* or the translator's book *The Heart of Buddhist Meditation.* Also a knowledge of the Buddha's original "Discourse on the Foundations of Mindfulness" (Satipaṭṭhāna Sutta) will be indispensable.

This treatise was first written in the Burmese language and later, in 1950, a Pali version of it was composed by the author. As the treatise deals chiefly with the advanced stages of the practice, it was originally not intended for publication.

Hand-written or typed copies of the Burmese or Pali version were given only to those who, with some measure of success, had concluded a strict course of practice at the meditation centre. For the use of meditators from foreign countries, only a few cyclostyled sheets in English, briefly describing the phases of insight knowledge, were issued instead of the treatise itself. This was done to enable the meditator to identify his personal experience with one or other of the stages described, so that he might direct his further progress accordingly, without being diverted or misled by any secondary phenomena that may have appeared during his practice.

In 1954 the Venerable Author agreed to a printed edition of the Pali version in Burmese script, and after this first publication he also permitted, at the translator's request, the issue of an English version. He had the great kindness to go carefully through the draft translation and the Notes, with the linguistic help of an experienced Burmese lay meditator, U Pe Thin, who for many years had ably served as an interpreter for meditators from foreign countries. The translator's gratitude is due to both his Venerable Meditation Master, the author, and to U Pe Thin.

NYANAPONIKA THERA

Forest Hermitage
Kandy, Ceylon,
On the Full-moon Day of June (Poson) 1965.

Homage to the Blessed One, the Worthy One,
the Fully Enlightened One

THE PROGRESS OF INSIGHT

Introduction

Homage to Him, the Great Omniscient Sage,
Who spread the net of rays of His Good Law!
These rays of His Good Law—His very message true—
Long may they shed their radiance o'er the world!

This treatise explains the progress of insight,[1] together
with the corresponding stages of purification.[2] It has been
written in brief for the benefit of meditators who have
obtained distinctive results in their practice, so that they may
more easily understand their experience. It is meant for those
who, in their practice of insight, have taken up as their main
subject either the tactile bodily process of motion,[3] evident
in the rising and falling movement of the abdomen,[4] or the
tactile bodily process based on three of the primary elements
of matter[5] evident in the sensation of touch (bodily impact).
It is meant for those who, by attending to these exercises,
have gained progressive insight as well into the whole body
and mind process arising at the six sense doors,[6] and have
finally come to see the Dhamma, to attain to the Dhamma,
to understand the Dhamma, to penetrate the Dhamma, who
have passed beyond doubt, freed themselves from

uncertainty, obtained assurance, and achieved independence of others in the Master's dispensation.[7]

I. PURIFICATION OF CONDUCT

Purification of conduct means here, in the case of male and female devotees *(upāsakas* and *upāsikās)*, the acceptance of the precepts, and the proper guarding and protecting of their observance—whether it be the Five Precepts, the Eight Uposatha Precepts, or the Ten Precepts.[8]

In the case of bhikkhus, purification of conduct is the well-kept purity of the fourfold conduct incumbent upon monks, beginning with restraint according to the disciplinary rules of bhikkhus, called the Pātimokkha. Of that fourfold conduct, the restraint according to the Pātimokkha rules is of first importance, because only when that restraint is pure will one be able to accomplish the development of meditation.[9]

The Method of Insight in Brief

There are two kinds of meditation development, tranquillity *(samatha)* and insight *(vipassanā)*. A person who, of these two, has first developed tranquillity, and after having established himself in either access concentration or full concentration,[10] subsequently contemplates the five groups of grasping,[11] is called a *samatha-yānika,* "one who has tranquillity as his vehicle."

As to his method of attaining insight, the *Papañcasūdanī,* commenting on the Dhammadāyāda Sutta of the Majjhima Nikāya, says: "Herein, a certain person first produces access concentration or full concentration; this is tranquillity. He then applies insight to that concentration and to the mental states associated with it, seeing them as impermanent, etc.; this is insight." In the *Visuddhimagga,* too, it is said: "He whose vehicle is tranquillity should first emerge from any fine-material or immaterial jhāna, except the base consisting of neither-perception-nor-non-perception, and he should then discern, according to characteristic, function, etc., the jhāna factors consisting of applied thought, etc., and the mental states associated with them" *(Path of Purification,* XVIII.3).

He, however, who has neither produced access concentration nor full concentration, but from the very start applies insight to the five groups of grasping, is called *suddha-vipassanā-yānika,*[12] "one who has pure insight as his vehicle." As to his method of attaining insight, it is said in the same Commentary to the Dhammadāyāda Sutta: "There is another person, who even without having produced the aforesaid tranquillity, applies insight to the five groups of grasping, seeing them as impermanent, etc." In the *Visuddhimagga,* too, it is said thus: "One who has pure insight as his vehicle ... contemplates the four elements."

In the Susīma-paribbājaka Sutta of the Nidānavagga Saṃyutta, too, it is said by the Buddha: "First arises the knowledge comprehending the actual happening of things *(dhammaṭṭhiti-ñāṇa)* and afterwards arises the knowledge realising Nibbāna *(nibbāne ñāṇa)."*

When purification of conduct has been established, the meditator who has chosen pure insight as his vehicle should endeavour to contemplate the body and mind *(nāma-rūpa).* In doing so, he should contemplate, according to their characteristics,[13] the five groups of grasping, that is, the bodily and mental processes that become evident to him in his own life-continuity (at his own six sense doors).[14]

Insight must, in fact, be developed by noticing,[15] according to their specific and general characteristics,[16] the bodily and mental processes that become evident at the six sense doors. In the beginning, however, it is difficult to follow and to notice clearly all bodily and mental processes that incessantly appear at the six sense doors. Therefore the meditator who is a beginner should first notice the perfectly distinct process of touch, perceived through the door of bodily sensitivity; because the *Visuddhimagga* says that in insight meditation one should take up what is distinct. When sitting, there occurs the bodily process of touch by way of the sitting posture and through touch sensitivity in the body. These processes of tactile sensitivity should be noticed as "Sitting ... touching ...," and so forth, in due succession. Further, at the seated meditator's abdomen, the tactile process of bodily motion (that is, the wind, or vibratory, element) which has breathing as its condition, is perceptible continuously as the rise (expansion) and fall (contraction) of the abdomen. That too should be noticed as "rising, falling," and so forth. While the meditator is thus engaged in noticing the element of motion which impinges continuously on the door of bodily sensitivity in the abdomen, it becomes evident to him in its aspects of stiffening, of vibrating, and of pushing and pulling. Here, the aspect of stiffening shows the motion element's *characteristic nature* of supporting; the aspect of vibrating shows its *essential function* of movement; and the aspect of pushing and pulling shows its *manifestation* of impelling.[17]

Hence the meditator, noticing the tactile bodily process of rise and fall of the abdomen, accomplishes the observation of the bodily process *(rūpa),* by getting to know the characteristic nature, etc., of the element of motion. Later when he has accomplished the observation of mind *(nāma)* and the observation of both body and mind *(nāma-rūpa),* he will also come to know the *general* characteristics of the processes concerned—their impermanence, liability to suffering, and their being void of a self.

But while he is engaged in just noticing the rising and falling of the abdomen and other tactile processes, there will appear thoughts of desire, etc., feelings of pleasure, etc., or acts such as adjusting various parts of the body. At that time, these activities (of mind and body) must be noticed, too. After noticing them, he should turn again to the continuous noticing of the tactile process of the rising and falling of the abdomen, which is the basic object of mindfulness in this practice.

This is a brief sketch of the methodical practice of insight. It is not the place here to treat it in detail, because this is a brief essay on the progress of insight through the stages of purification; it is not a treatise explaining in detail the methodical practice of insight.

II. THE PURIFICATION OF MIND

During the early part of the methodical practice, as long as the meditator's mind is not yet fully purified, wandering thoughts arisen by his thinking of objects of sense desire, etc., will also appear intermittently between thoughts of noticing (the objects of meditation). Sometimes the beginning meditator will perceive occurrence (of these interruptions) and sometimes he will not. But even if he perceives them, it will be only after a short time has elapsed after their appearance. For then the momentary concentration of his mind is still very tender and weak. So these wandering thoughts continue to hinder his mind while it is occupied in developing the practice of noticing. Hence, these wandering thoughts are called "hindering thoughts."

When, however, the momentary concentration of his mind has become strong, the thought process of noticing becomes well concentrated. Hence, when attending to the objects to be noticed—the abdominal movement, sitting, touching, bending, stretching, seeing, hearing, etc.—his noticing thoughts now appear as if falling upon these objects, as if striking at them, as if confronting them again and again. Then, as a rule, his mind will no longer go elsewhere. Only occasionally, and in a slight degree, will this happen, and even in those cases he will be able to notice any such stray thought at its very arising, as expressed in common speech; or, to be exact, he will notice the stray thought immediately after its actual arising. Then that stray thought will subside as soon as it is noticed and will not arise again. Immediately afterwards he will also be able to resume continuous noticing of any object as it becomes evident to him. That is why his mind at that time is called "unhindered."

While the meditator is thus practising the exercise of noticing with unhindered mind, the noticing mind will close in upon and fix on whatever object is being noticed, and the act of noticing will proceed without break. At that time there arises in him in uninterrupted succession "the concentration of mind lasting for a moment," directed to each object noticed. This is called *purification of mind.*[18]

Though that concentration has only momentary duration, its power of resistance to being overwhelmed by opposition corresponds to that of access concentration.

In the Commentary to the *Visuddhimagga*, in the explanation of the chapter relating to mindfulness of breathing, it is said thus: " 'Momentary unification of mind' means the concentration of mind lasting only for a moment. For that (type of concentration), too, when it occurs uninterruptedly with its respective object in a single mode and is not overcome by opposition, fixes the mind immovably, as if in absorption."

"It occurs uninterruptedly with its respective object" refers to the uninterrupted continuity of the thoughts engaged in noticing; after noticing one object, one attends, in the same manner, to another that follows immediately;[19] again, having noticed that object, one turns to the next one, and so on.

"In a single mode" means: though the objects to be noticed, as they present themselves, are numerous and varied, yet the force of concentration of the mind uninterruptedly engaged in noticing remains virtually on the same level. For what is meant here is: just as the first object was noticed with a certain degree of concentration, so the second, third, and other subsequent objects are noticed in each case with the same degree of concentration.

"Is not overcome by opposition": this means that the momentary concentration in its uninterrupted flow is not overwhelmed by the mental hindrances.[20]

"As if in absorption": this means that the strength of the momentary concentration is similar to that of concentration which has reached full mental absorption. However, such similarity of momentary concentration with fully absorbed concentration will become evident (only) when the methodical practice of insight reaches its culmination.[21]

But is it not said in the Commentaries that the term "purification of mind" applies only to access concentration and fully absorbed concentration? That is true; but one has to take this statement in the sense that momentary concentration is included in access concentration. For in the Commentary to the Satipaṭṭhāna Sutta it is said: "The remaining twelve exercises are subjects of meditation leading only to Access Concentration."[22] Now, in the case of the subjects dealt with in the sections of the Satipaṭṭhāna Sutta on postures, clear comprehension and elements, the concentration of one who devotes himself to these exercises will be definitely only momentary concentration. But, as the latter is able to suppress the hindrances just as access concentration does,[23] and since it is in the neighbourhood of the noble-path attainment concentration,[24] therefore that same momentary concentration is spoken of by the name of "access" (or "neighbourhood") and also the meditation subjects that produce that momentary concentration are called "meditation subjects leading to access concentration." Hence it should be understood that momentary concentration, having the capacity to suppress the hindrances, has also the right to the name "access" and "purification of mind." Otherwise purification of mind could not come about in one who has made bare insight his vehicle by employing only insight, without having produced either access concentration or fully absorbed concentration.

III. PURIFICATION OF VIEW

1. Analytical Knowledge of Body and Mind

Endowed with purification of mind and continuing the practice of noticing, the meditator now comes to know body and mind analytically as follows: "The rising (upward movement) of the abdomen is one process; the falling (downward movement) is another; sitting is another; touching is another," etc. In this way he comes to know how to distinguish each bodily process that he notices. Further he realises: "The knowing of the rising movement is one process; the knowing of the falling movement is another." In that way he comes to know each mental act of noticing. Further he realises: "The rising movement is one process; the knowing of it is another. The falling movement is one process; the knowing of it is another," and so on. In that way he comes to know how to distinguish each bodily and mental process. All that knowledge comes from simply noticing, not from reasoning; that is to say, it is knowledge by direct experience arrived at by the mere act of noticing, and not knowledge derived from ratiocination.

Thus, when seeing a visual object with the eye, the meditator knows how to distinguish each single factor involved: "The eye is one; the visual object is another; seeing is another, and knowing it is another." The same manner applies in the case of the other sense functions.

For at the time, in each act of noticing, the meditator comes to know analytically the mental processes of noticing, and those of thinking and reflecting, knowing them for himself through direct knowledge by his experience thus: "They have the nature of going towards an object, inclining towards an object, cognising an object." On the other hand, he knows analytically the material processes going on in the whole body—which are here described as "the rising and falling movements of the abdomen," "sitting," etc., knowing them thus: "These have *not* the nature of going or inclining towards an object, or of cognising an object." Such knowing is called "knowing matter (or the body) by its manifestation of non-determining." For it is said in the *Mūla-ṭīkā*, the "Principal Sub-commentary" to the Vibhaṅga: "In other words, 'non-determining' (as in the passage quoted) should be understood as having no faculty of cognising an object."

Such knowledge as this, which analyses in each act of noticing both the bodily process noticed and the mental process engaged in noticing, according to their true essential nature, is called "analytical knowledge of body and mind."

When that knowledge has come to maturity, the meditator understands thus: "At the moment of breathing in, there is just the rising movement of the abdomen and the knowing of the movement, but there is no self besides; at the moment of breathing out, there is just the falling movement of the abdomen and the knowing of the movement, but there is no self besides." Understanding it thus in these and other instances, he knows and sees for himself by noticing thus: "There is here only that pair: a material process as object, and a mental process of knowing it; and it is to that pair alone that the terms of conventional usage 'being,' 'person' or 'soul,' 'I' or 'another,' 'man' or 'woman' refer. But apart from that dual process there is no separate person or being, I or another, man or woman."

This is called *purification of view.*

IV. PURIFICATION BY OVERCOMING DOUBT

2. Knowledge by Discerning Conditionality

When purification of view has come to maturity, the conditions necessary for the bodily and mental processes observed will also become evident. Firstly, the consciousness that is the condition of the (respective) bodily process will be evident. How? For instance, when bending the arms or legs, the consciousness intending to bend these limbs is evident. So the meditator first notices that consciousness, and next he notices the act of bending, and so on. Then he understands by direct experience: "When there is consciousness intending to bend a limb, the bodily process of bending arises; when there is consciousness intending to stretch a limb, the bodily process of stretching arises." And in the same way he understands other instances too by direct experience.

Again, he also understands by direct experience the condition for the mental process, in the following manner: "In the case of consciousness desirous of running off the track, there arises first a corresponding consciousness giving initial attention (to the distracting object). If that consciousness is not noticed (with mindfulness), then there arises a consciousness that runs off the track. But if the consciousness of initial attention to the distracting object is noticed and known, no stray thought will arise. It is similar in the case of other types of consciousness (for instance, when taking delight or being angry, greedy, etc.). When both the sense door of the eye and a visual object are present, there arises visual consciousness; otherwise visual consciousness will not arise; and so it is in the case of the other sense doors. If there is a noticeable or recognisable object, then there arises consciousness engaged in noticing or thinking or reasoning or understanding, as the case may be; otherwise no such consciousness arises. Similarly he understands what occurs in every other instance (of mind-door cognition).

At that time, the meditator will generally experience many different painful feelings arising in his body. Now, while one of these feelings is being noticed (but without concern), another feeling will arise elsewhere; and while that is being noticed, again another will appear elsewhere. Thus the meditator follows each feeling as it arises and notices it. But though he is engaged in noticing these feelings as they arise, he will only perceive their initial phase of "arising" and not their final phase of "dissolution."

Also many mental images of various shapes will then appear. The shape of a dagoba, a monk, a man, a house, a tree, a park, a heavenly mansion, a cloud, and many other such images will appear. Here, too, while the meditator is still engaged in noticing one of these mental images, another will show itself; while still noticing that, yet another will appear. Following thus the mental images as they arise, he goes on noticing them. But though he is engaged in noticing them, he will perceive only their initial phase, not the final phase.

He now understands: "Consciousness arises in accordance with each object that becomes evident. If there is an object, there arises consciousness; if there is no object, no consciousness arises."

Between sequences of noticing he also, by considering inferentially, comes to know thus: "It is due to the presence of such causes and conditions as ignorance, craving, kamma, etc., that body and mind continue."

Such discernment through direct experience and through inference as described, when noticing body and mind with their conditions, is called "knowledge of discerning conditionality."

When that knowledge has come to maturity, the meditator perceives only body and mind processes occurring in strict accordance with their particular and appropriate conditions and he comes to the conclusion: "Here is only a conditioning body and mind process and a conditioned body and mind process. Apart from these, there is no person who performs the bending of the limbs, etc., or who experiences feelings of pain, etc."

This is called *purification (of insight) by overcoming doubt.*

3. Knowledge of Comprehension

When this "purification (of insight) by overcoming doubt" has reached maturity, the meditator will discern distinctly the initial, middle, and final phases of any object noticed by him. Then, in the case of various objects noticed, he will discern distinctly that only after each earlier process has ceased, does there arise a subsequent process. For instance, only when the rising movement of the abdomen has come to an end, does there arise the falling movement; only when that has ended, is there again a rising movement. So also in the case of walking: only when the lifting of the foot has come to an end, does there arise the carrying forward of the foot; only when that has been completed, does there follow the placing of the foot on the ground.

In the case of painful feelings, only after each single feeling occurring at its particular place has ceased, will another new feeling arise at another place. On noticing the respective painful feeling repeatedly, twice, thrice or more, the meditator will see that it gradually grows less, and at last ceases entirely.

In the case of the variously shaped images that enter the mind's field, it is only after each single image noticed has vanished, that another new object will come into the mind's focus. On noticing them attentively twice, thrice or more, he will see well that these mental objects which are being noticed move from one place to another, or they become gradually smaller and less distinct, until at last they disappear entirely. The meditator, however, does not perceive anything that is permanent and lasting, or free from destruction and disappearance.

Seeing how each object, even while being noticed, comes to destruction and disappearance, the meditator comprehends it as *impermanent* in the sense of undergoing destruction. He further comprehends it as *suffering* (painful) in the sense of breaking up after each arising. Having seen how various painful feelings arise in continuous succession—how if one painful feeling ceases, another arises, and when that has ceased, again another arises—having seen that, he comprehends the respective objects as just a conglomeration of suffering. Further, he comprehends the object as consisting of mere *impersonal* phenomena without a master, in the sense of not arising of (or by) themselves, but arising subject to conditions and then breaking up.

This comprehension of an object noticed, as being imper—manent, painful, and without a self (impersonal), through knowing its impermanent nature, etc., by means of simply noticing, without reflecting and reasoning, is called "knowledge by comprehension through direct experience."

Having thus seen the three characteristics once or several times by direct experience, the meditator, by inference from the direct experience of those objects noticed, comprehends all bodily and mental processes of the past, present, and future, and the whole world, by coming to the conclusion: "They, too, are in the same way impermanent, painful, and without a self." This is called "knowledge of comprehension by inference."

Alluding to this very knowledge, it is said in the *Paṭisambhidāmagga:* "Whatever there is of materiality, past, present or future, internal or external, coarse or fine, inferior or superior, far or near, all materiality he defines as impermanent. That is one kind of comprehension," and so on.

Also in the Commentary to the *Kathāvatthu* it is said: "Even if the impermanence of only a single formation (conditioned phenomenon) is known, there may be consideration of the rest by induction thus: 'All formations are impermanent.'"

The words "All formations are impermanent" refer to an understanding by induction, and not to an understanding by perceiving a (co-present) object at the same moment. (This passage is the authority for the usage of the term "inductive insight.")

Also in the Commentary to the Majjhima Nikāya[25] it is said: "Because in the case of the realm of neither-perception-nor-non-perception, the insight into the sequence of mental factors belongs to the Buddhas alone and not to the disciples, he (the Buddha) said thus thereby indicating the insight by groups. " (This passage is the authority for the usage of the term "comprehension by groups.")[26]

4. Knowledge of Arising and Passing Away: The Ten Corruptions of Insight[27]

When the meditator, in the exercise of noticing, is able to keep exclusively to the present body and mind process, without looking back to past processes or ahead to future ones, then, as a result of insight, (the mental vision of) a *brilliant light* will appear to him. To one it will appear like the light of a lamp, to others like a flash of lightning, or like the radiance of the moon or the sun, and so on. With one it may last for just one moment, with others it may last longer.

There will also arise in him strong *mindfulness* pertaining to insight. As a result, all the successive arisings of bodily and mental processes will present themselves to the consciousness engaged in noticing, as if coming to it of themselves; and mindfulness too seems as if alighting on the processes of itself. Therefore the meditator then believes: "There is no body and mind process in which mindfulness fails to engage."

His *knowledge* consisting in insight, here called "noticing," will be likewise keen, strong, and lucid. Consequently, he will discern clearly and in separate forms all the bodily and mental processes noticed, as if cutting to pieces a bamboo sprout with a well-sharpened knife. Therefore the meditator then believes: "There is no body and mind process that cannot be noticed."

When examining the characteristics of impermanence, etc., or other aspects of reality, he understands everything quite clearly and at once, and he believes it to be the knowledge derived from direct experience.

Further, strong *faith* pertaining to insight arises in him. Under its influence, the meditator's mind, when engaged in noticing or thinking, is serene and without any disturbance; and when he is engaged in recollecting the virtues of the Buddha, the Dhamma, and the Sangha, his mind quite easily gives itself over to them. There arise in him the wish to proclaim the Buddha's Teaching, joyous confidence in the virtues of those engaged in meditation, the desire to advise dear friends and relatives to practise meditation, grateful remembrance of the help received from his meditation master, his spiritual mentor, etc. These and many other similar mental processes will occur.

There arises also *rapture* in its five grades, beginning with minor rapture.[28] When purification of mind is gained, that rapture begins to appear by causing "goose-flesh," tremor in the limbs, etc.; and now it produces a sublime feeling of happiness and exhilaration, filling the whole body with an exceedingly sweet and subtle thrill. Under its influence, he feels as if the whole body had risen up and remained in the air without touching the ground, or as if it were seated on an air cushion, or as if it were floating up and down.

There arises *tranquillity* of mind with the characteristic of quietening the disturbances of consciousness and its mental concomitants; and along with it appear mental agility, etc.[29] When walking, standing, sitting, or reclining there is, under the influence of these mental qualities, no disturbance of consciousness and its mental concomitants, nor heaviness, rigidity, unwieldiness, sickness, or crookedness.[30] Rather, his consciousness and its mental concomitants are tranquil through having reached the supreme relief in non-action.[31] They are agile in always functioning swiftly; they are pliant in being able to attend to any object desired; they are wieldy, in being able to attend to an object for any length of time desired; they are quite lucid through their proficiency, that is, through the ease with which insight penetrates the object; they are also straight through being directed, inclined, and turned only towards wholesome activities.

There also arises a very sublime feeling of *happiness* suffusing all his body. Under its influence he becomes exceedingly joyous and he believes: "Now I am happy all the time," or "Now, indeed, I have found happiness never felt before," and he wants to tell others of his extraordinary experience. With reference to that rapture and happiness, which are aided by the factors of tranquillity, etc., it was said:

> *Superhuman is the bliss of a monk*
> *Who, with mind at peace,*
> *Having entered a secluded place,*
> *Wins insight into Dhamma.*
> *When he fully comprehends*
> *The five groups' rise and fall,*
> *He wins to rapture and to joy—*
> *The Deathless this, for those who understand.*

Dhammapada *vv. 373-374*

There arises in him *energy* that is neither too lax nor too tense but is vigorous and acts evenly. For formerly his energy was sometimes lax, and so he was overpowered by sloth and torpor; hence he could not notice keenly and continuously the objects as they became evident, and his understanding, too, was not clear. And at other times his energy was too tense, and so he was overpowered by agitation, with the same result of being unable to notice keenly, etc. But now his energy is neither too lax nor too tense, but is vigorous and acts evenly; and so, overcoming these shortcomings of sloth, torpor, and agitation, he is able to notice the objects present keenly and continuously, and his understanding is quite clear, too.

There also arises in him strong *equanimity* associated with insight; which is neutral towards all formations. Under its influence he regards with neutrality even his examination of the nature of these formations with respect to their being impermanent, etc.; and he is able to notice keenly and continuously the bodily and mental processes arising at the time. Then his activity of noticing is carried on without effort, and proceeds, as it were, of itself. Also in adverting to the objects, there arises in him strong equanimity, by virtue of which his mind enters, as it were, quickly into the objects of advertence.[32]

There arises further a subtle *attachment* of a calm nature that enjoys the insight graced with the "brilliant light" and the other qualities here described. The meditator, however, is not able to discern it as a corruption but believes it to be just the very bliss of meditation. So meditators speak in praise of it thus: "Only now do I find full delight in meditation!"

Having felt such rapture and happiness accompanied by the "brilliant light" and enjoying the very act of perfect noticing, which is ably functioning with ease and rapidity, the meditator now believes: "Surely I must have attained to the supramundane path and fruition![33] Now I have finished the task of meditation." This is mistaking what is not the path for the path, and it is a corruption of insight which usually takes place in the manner just described. But even if the meditator does not take the "brilliant light" and the other corruptions as an indication of the path and fruition, still he feels delight in them. This is likewise a corruption of insight. Therefore, the knowledge consisting in noticing, even if quick in its functioning, is called "the early stage of (or 'weak') knowledge of arising and passing away," if it is beset and corrupted by those corruptions. For the same reason the meditator is at that time not in a position to discern quite distinctly the arising and passing away of bodily and mental processes.

V. PURIFICATION BY KNOWLEDGE AND VISION OF WHAT IS PATH AND NOT-PATH

While engaged in noticing, the meditator either by himself or through instructions from someone else, comes to this decision: "The brilliant light, and the other things experienced by me, are not the path. Delight in them is merely a corruption of insight. The practice of continuously noticing the object as it becomes evident—that alone is the way of insight. I must go on with just the work of noticing." This decision is called purification by knowledge and vision of what is path and not-path.

VI. PURIFICATION BY KNOWLEDGE AND VISION OF THE COURSE OF PRACTICE

After noticing these manifestations of brilliant light and the others, or after leaving them unheeded, he goes on continuously as before with the act of noticing the bodily and mental processes as they become evident at the six sense doors. While thus engaged in noticing, he gets over the corruptions relating to brilliant light, rapture, tranquillity, happiness, attachment, etc., and his knowledge remains concerned exclusively with the arising and passing away of the processes noticed. For then, at each act of noticing, he sees: "The noticed object, having arisen, disappears instantly." It also becomes clear to him that each object disappears just where it arises; it does not move on to another place.

In that way he understands by direct experience how bodily and mental processes arise and break up from moment to moment. It is such knowledge and understanding resulting from the continuous noticing of bodily and mental processes as they arise and dissolve moment after moment, and the discernment, in separate sections, of the arising and passing away of each of them, while being free from the corruptions, that is called "final knowledge of contemplation of arising and passing away." This is the beginning of "purification by knowledge and vision of the course of practice," which starts from this insight and extends to adaptation knowledge (No. 13).

5. Knowledge of Dissolution

Noticing the bodily and mental processes as they arise, he sees them part by part, link by link, piece by piece, fraction by fraction: "Just now it arises, just now it dissolves." When that knowledge of arising and passing away becomes mature, keen and strong, it will arise easily and proceed uninterruptedly as if borne onward of itself; also the bodily and mental processes will be easily discernible. When keen knowledge thus carries on and formations are easily discernible, then neither the arising of each bodily and mental process, nor its middle phase called "presence," nor the continuity of bodily and mental processes called "occurrence as unbroken flux" is apparent to him; nor are the shape of the hand, the foot, the face, the body, and so on, apparent to him. But what is apparent to him is only the *ceasing* of bodily and mental processes, called "vanishing," or "passing away," or "dissolution."

For instance, while noticing the rising movement of the abdomen, neither its initial nor middle phase is apparent, but only the ceasing or vanishing, which is called the final phase, is apparent; and so it is also with the falling movement of the abdomen. Again, in the case of bending an arm or leg, while noticing the act of bending, neither the initial nor the middle phase of bending is apparent, nor is the form of the limb apparent, but only the final phase of ceasing and vanishing is apparent. It is similar in the other cases of stretching a limb, and so on.

For at that time each object that is being noticed seems to him to be entirely absent or to have become non-existent. Consequently, at this stage of knowledge, it seems to him as if he were engaged in noticing something which has already become absent or non-existent by having vanished; and the consciousness engaged in noticing appears to have lost contact with the object that is being noticed. It is for that reason that a meditator may here think: "I have lost the insight"; but he should not think so.

For formerly his consciousness normally took delight in conceptual objects of shapes, etc.;[34] and even up to the knowledge of arising and passing away, the idea of formations with their specific features[35] was always apparent to him. Hence his mind took delight in a plainly distinguishable object consisting of formations, with its particular structure[36] and its particular feature-idea. But now that his knowledge has developed in the way described, no such idea of the formations' features or structure appears to him, still less any other, cruder concept. At such a stage, the *arising* of formations, that is, the first phase of the process, is not apparent (as it is in the case of knowledge of arising and passing away), but there is apparent only the dissolution, that is, the final phase, having the nature of vanishing. Therefore the meditator's mind does not take delight in it at first, but he may be sure that soon, after becoming familiar (with that stage of the practice), his mind will delight in the cessation (of the phenomena) too, which is called their dissolution. With this assurance he should again turn to the practice of continuous noticing.

When thus engaged, he perceives that in each act of noticing there are always present two factors, an objective factor and a subjective one—the object noticed and the mental state of knowing it—which dissolve and vanish by pairs, one pair after the other. For in each single instance of a rising movement of the abdomen, there are, in fact, numerous physical processes constituting the rising movement, which are seen to dissolve serially. It is like seeing the continuous successive vanishing of a summer mirage moment by moment; or it is like the quick and continuous bursting of bubbles produced in a heavy shower by thick rain drops falling on a water surface; or it is like the quick, successive extinguishing of oil-lamps blown out by wind at the time of offering lamps to a stupa. Similar to that appears the dissolving and vanishing, moment by moment, of the bodily processes noticed. And the dissolution of consciousness noticing those bodily processes is apparent to him along with the dissolution of the bodily processes. Also while he is noticing other bodily and mental processes, their dissolution, too, will be apparent to him in the same manner. Consequently, the knowledge will come to him that whatever part of the whole body is noticed, that object ceases first, and after it the consciousness engaged in noticing that object follows in its wake. From that the meditator will understand very clearly in the case of each successive pair the dissolution of any object whatsoever and the dissolution of the consciousness noticing that very object. (It should be borne in mind that this refers only to understanding arrived at through direct experience by one engaged in noticing only; it is not an opinion derived from mere reasoning.)

It is the perfectly clear understanding of the dissolution of the two things, pair by pair—that is, (1) of the visual or other object appearing at any of the six sense doors, and (2) of the consciousness noticing that very object—that is called "knowledge of dissolution."

6. Awareness of Fearfulness

When that knowledge of dissolution is mature, there will gradually arise, just by seeing the dissolution of all object-and-subject-formations, awareness of fearfulness[37] and other (higher) knowledges, together with their respective aspects of fear, and so on.[38]

Having seen how the dissolution of two things—that is, any object noticed and the insight-thought engaged in noticing it—takes place moment by moment, the meditator also understands by inference that in the past, too, every conditioned thing (formation) has broken up in the same way, that just so it will break up also in the future, and that at the present it breaks up, too. And just at the time of noticing any formations that are evident, these formations will appear to him in their aspect of fearfulness. Therefore, during the very act of noticing, the meditator will also come to understand: "These formations are indeed fearful."

Such understanding of their fearfulness is called "knowledge of the awareness of fearfulness"; it has also the name "knowledge of fear." At that time, his mind itself is gripped by fear and seems helpless.

7. Knowledge of Misery

When he has realised the fearfulness (of the formations) through the knowledge of fear, and keeps on noticing continuously, then the "knowledge of misery" will arise in him before long. When it has arisen, all formations everywhere—whether among the objects noticed, or among the states of consciousness engaged in noticing, or in any kind of life or existence that is brought to mind—will appear insipid, without a vitalising factor,[39] and unsatisfying. So he sees, at that time, only suffering, only unsatisfactoriness, only misery. Therefore this state is called "knowledge of misery."

8. Knowledge of Disgust

Seeing thus the misery in conditioned things (formations), his mind finds no delight in those miserable things but is entirely disgusted with them. At times, his mind becomes, as it were, discontented and listless. Even so he does not give up the practice of insight, but spends his time continuously engaging in it. He therefore should know that this state of mind is not dissatisfaction with meditation, but is precisely the "knowledge of disgust". that has the aspect of being disgusted with the formations. Even if he directs his thought to the happiest sort of life and existence, or to the most pleasant and desirable objects, his mind will not take delight in them, will find no satisfaction in them. On the contrary, his mind will incline and lean and tend only towards Nibbāna. Therefore the following thought will arise in him between moments of noticing: "The ceasing of all formations that are dissolving from moment to moment—that alone is happiness."

9. Knowledge of Desire for Deliverance

When through this knowledge (now acquired) he feels disgust with regard to every formation noticed, there will arise in him a desire to forsake these formations or to become delivered from them. The knowledge relating to that desire is called "knowledge of desire for deliverance." At that time, usually various painful feelings arise in his body, and also an unwillingness to remain long in one particular bodily posture. Even if these states do not arise, the comfortless nature of the formations will become more evident than ever. And due to that, between moments of noticing, he feels a longing thus: "Oh, may I soon get free from that! Oh, may I reach the state where these formations cease! Oh, may I be able to give up these formations completely!" At this juncture, his consciousness engaged in noticing seems to shrink from the object noticed at each moment of noticing, and wishes to escape from it.

10. Knowledge of Re-observation

Being thus desirous of escaping from the formations, the meditator makes stronger effort and continues the practice of noticing these very formations with the single purpose of forsaking them and escaping from them. For that reason, the knowledge arising at that time is called "knowledge of re-observation." The term "re-observation" has the same meaning as "re-noticing" or "re-contemplation." Then the nature (or characteristics) of the formations—their being impermanent, suffering, and without a self—will be clearly evident to him; and among these three, the aspect of suffering will be particularly distinct.

At this stage, too, there will usually arise in his body various kinds of pains which are severe, sharp, and of growing intensity. Hence his whole bodily and mental system will seem to him like an unbearable mass of sickness or a conglomeration of suffering. And a state of restlessness will usually manifest itself, making him incapable of keeping to one particular posture for any length of time. For then he will not be able to hold any one position long, but will soon want to change it. This state, however, simply manifests the unbearable nature of the formations. Though he wants to change his bodily posture, still he should not give in easily to that wish, but should endeavour to remain motionless for a longer period in the same posture and continue to carry on the practice of noticing. By doing so he will be able to overcome his restlessness.

Now his insight knowledge is quite strong and lucid, and by virtue of it even his painful feelings will at once cease as soon as they are firmly noticed. Even if a painful feeling does not cease completely, he will perceive that it is dissolving, part by part, from moment to moment. That is to say, the ceasing, vanishing, and disappearing of each single moment of feeling will become apparent separately in each corresponding act of noticing. In other words, now it will not be as it was at the time of the knowledge of comprehension, when the constant flow or continuity of feelings of the same kind was apparent as a single unit. But if, without abandoning the practice, that feeling of pain is firmly and continuously noticed, it will entirely cease before long. When it ceases in that way, it does so for good and will not arise again. Though in that way the insight knowledge may have become strong and perfectly lucid, still he is not satisfied with that much. He will even think: "My insight knowledge is not clear." He should, however, dismiss such thoughts by applying the act of noticing to them, and he should go on with his task of continuously noticing the bodily and mental formations as they occur.

If he perseveres thus, his noticing will become more and more clear as the time passes in minutes, hours, and days. Then he will overcome the painful feelings and the restlessness in being unable to remain long in one particular posture, and also the idea that his insight knowledge is not yet clear enough. His noticing will then function rapidly, and at every moment of noticing he will understand quite clearly any of the three characteristics of impermanence, etc.

This understanding of any of the three characteristics of impermanence, etc., through the act of noticing which functions with promptness in quick succession, is called "strong knowledge of re-observation."

11. Knowledge of Equanimity about Formations

When this knowledge of re-observation is mature, there will arise knowledge perceiving evident bodily and mental processes in continuous succession quite naturally, as if borne onward of itself. This is called "knowledge of equanimity about formations."

Now, in the act of noticing, effort is no longer required to keep formations before the mind or to understand them. After the completion of each single act of noticing, the object to be noticed will then appear of itself, and insight knowledge, too, will of itself notice and understand it. It is as if no further effort need be made by the meditator. Formerly, owing to seeing the dissolution of formations, there arose, in successive order, the aspect of fearfulness, the perception of misery, the aspect of disgust, the desire for deliverance, and dissatisfaction with the knowledge so far acquired. But now these mental states no longer arise even though, in the present state too, the breaking up of formations which are dissolving more rapidly is closely perceived. Even if a painful feeling arises in the body, no mental disturbance (grief) arises, and there is no lack of fortitude in bearing it. Generally, however, at this stage, pains will be entirely absent, that is, they do not arise at all. Even if the meditator thinks about something fearful or sad, no mental disturbance will arise, be it in the form of fear or of sorrow. This, firstly, is "the abandoning of fear" at the stage of "equanimity about formations."

At the earlier stage, on attaining knowledge of arising and passing away, great joy had arisen on account of the clarity of insight. But now this kind of joy does not arise, even though there is present the exceedingly peaceful and sublime clarity of mind belonging to "equanimity about formations." Though he actually sees desirable objects conducive to joy, or though he thinks about various enjoyable things, no strong feeling of joy will arise. This is "the abandoning of delight" at the stage of "equanimity about formations."

He cherishes no desire nor hate with regard to any object, desirable or undesirable, that comes into the range of his sense doors, but taking them as just the same in his act of noticing, he understands them (that is to say, it is a pure act of understanding). This is "equable vision" at the stage of "equanimity about formations."

Of these three qualities just mentioned, it is said in the *Path of Purification:* "Having discarded fear and delight, he is impartial and neutral towards all formations" *(Visuddhimagga,* XXI.62).

If he resumes the practice of noticing with the thought: "Now I will do it vigorously again!" then, before long, the noticing will function efficiently as if borne onward of itself.

From now onwards there is no need for the meditator to make further (deliberate) effort. Though he does not make a (deliberate) effort, his noticing will proceed in a continuous and steady flow for a long time; it will go on even for two or three hours without interruption. This is "the state of long-lasting (practice)" of equanimity about formations. Referring to this it is said in the *Paṭisambhidāmagga:* " 'The wisdom lasting long' is the knowledge present in the mental states of equanimity about formations." The Great Commentary to the *Path of Purification* explains as follows: "This is said with reference to knowledge functioning in a continuous flow."

Now when noticing functions spontaneously as if borne onward of itself, the mind, even if sent out towards a variety of objects, generally refuses to go; and even if it does go, it will not stay long but will soon return to the usual object to be noticed, and will resume continuous noticing. In this connection it was said: "He shrinks, recoils, and retreats; he does not go forth to it."

12. Insight Leading to Emergence

So, through knowledge of equanimity about formations, which is endowed with many virtues, blessings, and powers, he notices the formations as they occur. When this knowledge is mature, having become keen, strong, and lucid, on reaching its culmination point, it will understand any of the formations as being impermanent or painful or without self, just by seeing their dissolution. Now that act of noticing any one characteristic out of the three, which is still more lucid in its perfect understanding, manifests itself two or three times or more in rapid succession. This is called "insight leading to emergence."[40]

Thereupon, immediately after the last consciousness in the series of acts of noticing belonging to this insight leading to emergence, the meditator's consciousness leaps forth into Nibbāna, which is the cessation of all formations, taking it as its object. Then there appears to him the stilling (subsidence) of all formations called cessation.

This mode of realisation of Nibbāna has been mentioned in many discourses of the Master, for example: "The vision of truth arose: whatsoever has the nature of arising is bound to cease." Herein the words "bound to cease" indicate the aspect of realising the stilling and ceasing of all formations which have the nature of arising.

Also in the *Questions of King Milinda* (Milindapañhā) it is said: "His consciousness, while carrying on the practice of bringing to mind (i.e., noticing), passes beyond the continuous occurrence of phenomena and alights upon non-occurrence. One who, having practised in the correct manner, has alighted upon non-occurrence, O king, is said to have realised Nibbāna."

The meaning is this: the meditator who wishes to realise Nibbāna should repeatedly bring to mind, through the practice of noticing, every bodily and mental process that appears at any of the six sense doors. When he brings them to mind thus, his consciousness engaged in noticing—here called "bringing to mind"—will, until adaptation knowledge is reached, fall at every moment upon the (conditioned) bodily and mental formations called here "continuous occurrence," because they go on occurring over and over again in an unbroken flow, like a river's current. But in the last phase, instead of falling upon that continuous occurrence, consciousness passes beyond it and alights upon "non-occurrence," which is the very opposite of the bodily and mental formations called here "occurrence." In other words, it arrives at non-occurrence, that is to say, it reaches, as if it "alights upon," cessation, which is the stilling of the formations (or conditioned phenomena). When the meditator, having already before practised correctly and without deviation by way of the knowledge of arising and passing away and the other knowledges (or by way of the purification of conduct, of mind, of view, etc.), has in this manner arrived at non-occurrence (by the consciousness alighting upon it), he is said to have "realised Nibbāna." He is called one who has made Nibbāna a direct experience and has actually seen it.

13. Knowledge of Adaptation

Here the knowledge by way of noticing that occurs last in the series constituting insight leading to emergence, is called "knowledge of adaptation."[41]

This is the end of the *purification by knowledge and vision of the course of practice.*

14. Maturity Knowledge

Immediately afterwards, a type of knowledge manifests itself that, as it were, falls for the first time into Nibbāna, which is void of formations (conditioned phenomena) since it is the cessation of them. This knowledge is called "maturity knowledge."[42]

VII. PURIFICATION BY KNOWLEDGE AND VISION

15. Path Knowledge

It is followed immediately by knowledge that abides in that same Nibbāna, which is void of formations since it is the cessation of them. This is called "path knowledge."[43] It is also called "purification by knowledge and vision."

16. Fruition Knowledge

That again is immediately followed by knowledge that belongs to the final stage and continues in the course of its predecessor. It abides in that same Nibbāna, which is void of formations since it is the cessation of them. This is called "fruition knowledge."

17. Knowledge of Reviewing

The duration of that threefold knowledge of maturity, path, and fruition is, however, not long. It is very short, and lasts for just an instant, like the duration of a single thought of noticing. Subsequently there arises "knowledge of reviewing." Through that knowledge of reviewing the meditator discerns that the insight leading to emergence came along with the very rapid function of noticing, and that immediately after the last phase of noticing, the path consciousness entered into the cessation (of formations). This is "knowledge reviewing the path."

He also discerns that the consciousness abided in that same state of cessation during the intervening period between the path and reviewing. This is "knowledge reviewing fruition."

He further discerns that the object just experienced is void of all formations. This is "knowledge reviewing Nibbāna."

In this connection it is said in the *Path of Purification:* " 'By that path, indeed, I have come'; thus he reviews the path. 'That blessing was obtained'; thus he reviews the fruition. 'That state has been penetrated as an object by me';[44] thus he reviews the Deathless, Nibbāna" *(Visuddhimagga,* xxii.20).

Some meditators, but not all, have "reviewing of defilements."[45]

After having reviewed in this way, the meditator still continues the practice of noticing bodily and mental processes as they become evident. But while he is thus engaged in noticing, the bodily and mental processes appear to him quite coarse, not subtle as before at the time of the knowledge of equanimity about formations. Why is this so? This is so because the knowledge present now has the nature of the knowledge of arising and passing away. For when the noble disciples (namely, stream-winners, etc.) resume the practice of insight (by noticing), the knowledge of arising and passing away usually arises at the beginning. This is the usual course of order in this respect.

However, when some meditators emerge from the attainment of path and fruition, great faith, happiness, rapture, and tranquillity, produced by virtue of the attainment, arise flooding the whole body. Owing to that, they are unable to carry out the practice of noticing anything apparent at that time. Even if they make double effort and attempt to proceed with the practice of insight, they fail to discern the phenomena clearly and separately, at the moment of their occurrence. They continue to experience only rapture, tranquillity, and happiness, which occur with great force. This state of mind, which is extraordinarily serene through the strong faith prevailing, lasts for one hour, two hours, or more, without break. Because of this, meditators feel as if they were in some such place as a wide open space suffused with radiance and most delightful. The rapture and happiness, of a serene character, that then arise are praised by meditators thus: "Surely, I have never before felt and experienced such happiness!" After two or three hours have passed, that faith, happiness, rapture, and tranquillity will fade. The meditators can once again proceed with noticing the bodily and mental processes as they occur, distinguishing them separately, and they will be able to discern them clearly. But at that time, too, first the knowledge of arising and passing away will appear.

18. Attainment of Fruition

While he is thus engaged in noticing, his insight knowledge will gradually grow, and soon will again reach the stage of equanimity about formations. If his power of concentration is still short of perfection, only the equanimity about formations will go on repeating itself. But if his concentration has reached perfection, then, in the case of one who does the insight practice of noticing with a view of attaining only to the first path and fruition, the fruition consciousness of the first path alone reaches cessation of formations by way of the *attainment of fruition*.[46] This occurs in precisely the same way as the path and fruition consciousness that occurred earlier in the consciousness-sequence belonging to the initial attainment of the first path. The only difference here is the capacity of the fruition attainment to last long.

One should also set one's mind resolutely upon the further tasks: to be able to repeat the achievement of fruition attainment, to achieve it rapidly, and, at the time of achievement, to abide in it a long time, say for six, ten, fifteen or thirty minutes, or for an hour or more.

In one who applies himself to achieving the attainment of fruition, knowledge of arising and passing away will arise at the beginning. Advancing from there in the due sequence, soon the knowledge of equanimity about formations is reached. But when skill in the practice has been acquired, the knowledge of equanimity about formations will arise quickly even after four or five acts of noticing. If the power of concentration has reached perfection, the fruition consciousness will repeatedly become absorbed in cessation by way of fruition attainment. The mind can thus reach absorption even while one is walking up and down, or while taking a meal, and the fruition attainment can remain for any length of time resolved upon. During the fruition attainment, the mind will abide only in the cessation of formations and will not be aware of anything else.

19. The Higher Paths and Fruitions

When the meditator has thus become skilled in achieving the fruition attainment, he should resolutely set his mind upon the task of attaining to the higher paths and fruitions. What should now be done by one who has set himself that task? Just as before, he should carry out the practice of noticing (anything occurring) at the six sense doors.

Hence, the meditator should notice any bodily and mental process that becomes evident to him at the six sense doors. While he is thus engaged, he will see, at the stage of knowledge of arising and passing away, that the first objects consisting of formations appear to him rather coarse, and that his mind is not well concentrated. The development of insight belonging to the higher paths is, in fact, not as easy as that of insight belonging to the fruition attainment already achieved by the meditator. It is in fact somewhat difficult, due to the fact that insight has to be developed anew. It is, however, not so very difficult as it was at the first time when beginning the practice. In a single day, or even in a single hour, he can gain the knowledge of equanimity about formations. This statement is made here, basing it on the experience usually gained by persons of the present day who had to be given guidance from the start and who did not possess particularly strong intelligence. Here it is applied, by inference, to similar types of persons in general.

But although equanimity about formations has been attained, if the spiritual faculties[47] have not yet reached full maturity, it just goes on repeating itself. Though he who has won (one of the lower) fruitions may be able to enter into it several times within one hour, yet if his spiritual faculties are immature, he cannot attain the next higher path within as much as one day, two, three, or more days. He abides merely in equanimity about formations. If, however, he then directs his mind to reach the fruition already attained, he will reach it perhaps in two or three minutes.

When, however, the spiritual faculties are mature, one who carries out the practice of insight for attaining to a higher path will find that immediately after equanimity about formations has reached its culmination, the higher path and fruition arise in the same way as before (i.e., as at the time of the first path and fruition), that is to say, it is preceded by the stages of adaptation and maturity. After the fruition, the stages of reviewing, etc., that follow are also the same as before.

Anything else concerning the method of practice for insight and the progress of knowledge right up to arahantship can be understood in precisely the same way as described. Hence there is no need to elaborate it any further.

Conclusion

Now, the present treatise on the "Progress of Insight through the Stages of Purification" has been written in a concise form, so that meditators can easily comprehend it. Hence complete details have not been given here. And since it was written with a view to making it easily intelligible, in many passages of this treatise relevant canonical references have not been quoted, and there are repetitions and other faults of literary composition. But these shortcomings of presentation and the incompleteness of canonical references may here be overlooked by the reader. Only the meaning and purpose should be heeded well by the wise. It is to this that I would invite the reader's attention.

Though in the beginning it was mentioned that this treatise has been written for those who have already obtained distinctive results in their practice, others may perhaps read it with advantage, too.

Now these are my concluding good wishes for the latter type of readers: Just as a very delicious, appetising, tasty and nutritious meal can be appreciated fully only by one who has himself eaten it, and not without partaking of it, in the same way, the whole series of knowledges described here can be understood fully only by one who has himself seen it by direct experience, and not otherwise. So may all good people reach the stage of indubitable understanding of this whole series of knowledges! May they also strive to attain it!

> *This treatise on the purities and insights,*
> *For meditators who have seen things clear,*
> *Although their store of learning may be small—*
> *The Elder, Mahāsi by name, in insight's method skillful,*
> *Has written it in Burmese tongue and into Pali rendered it.*

The Treatise on the Purities and Insights composed on 22.5.1950 is here concluded.

NOTES

1. Here, and in the title of this treatise, the Pali term *ñāṇa* has been rendered by "insight," as at the outset the word "knowledge," the normal rendering of *ñāṇa*, might not be taken by the reader with the full weight and significance which it will receive in the context of the present treatise. In all the following occurrences, however, this Pali term has been translated by "knowledge," while the word "insight" has been reserved for the Pali term *vipassanā*. When referring to the several types and stages of knowledge, the plural "knowledges" has been used, in conformity with the Pali *ñāṇāni*.

2. In the canonical Buddhist scriptures, the seven stages of purification *(visuddhi)* are mentioned in the Discourse on the Stage Coaches (Majjhima Nikāya No. 24). They are also the framework of the Venerable Buddhaghosa's *Path of Purification (Visuddhimagga),* where they are explained in full. (Translation by Ñāṇamoli Thera, published by BPS.)

3. "Motion" *(vāyo,* lit. wind, air) refers to the last of the four material elements *(dhātu),* or primary qualities of matter. The other three are: earth (solidity, hardness), water (adhesion), and fire (caloricity). These four elements, in varying proportional strength, are present in all forms of matter. The so-called "inner wind element" which applies in this context is active in the body as motion, vibration, and pressure manifesting itself in the passage of air through the body (e.g., in breathing), in the movement and pressure of limbs and organs, and so on. It becomes perceptible as a tactile process, or object of touch *(phoṭṭhabbārammaṇa),* through the pressure caused by it.

4. The attention directed to the movement of the abdomen was introduced into the methodical practice of insight-meditation by the author of this treatise, the Venerable Mahāsi Sayādaw,

and forms here the basic object of meditative practice. For details see *The Heart of Buddhist Meditation* by Nyānaponika Thera (London: Rider & Co., 1962; BPS, 1992), pp. 94f., 106. If preferred, the breath itself may instead be taken as the basic object of meditative attention, according to the traditional method of "mindfulness of breathing" *(ānāpānasati);* see *Heart of Buddhist Meditation,* pp.108ff. *Mindfulness of Breathing* by Ñāṇamoli Thera (BPS, 1982).

5. According to the Buddhist Abhidhamma teachings, only the three elements of earth, fire, and wind constitute the tactile substance in matter. The element of water is not held to be an object of touch even in cases where it predominates, as in liquids. What is tactile in any given liquid is the contribution of the other three elements to its composite nature.

6. "Door" is a figurative expression for the sense organs (which, including the mind, are sixfold), because they provide, as it were, the access to the world of objects.

7. The preceding sequence of terms is frequently used in the Discourses (Suttas) of the Buddha to refer to those individuals who have attained to the first supramundane stage on the road to arahantship, i.e., stream-entry *(sotāpatti),* or the following ones. See Note 33. The term *Dhamma* refers here to Nibbāna.

8. I. The Five Precepts binding on all Buddhist laymen, are: abstention from (1) killing, (2) stealing, (3) unlawful sexual intercourse, (4) lying, (5) intoxicants.

   II. The Eight Uposatha Precepts are: abstention from (1) killing, (2) stealing, (3) all sexual intercourse, (4) lying, (5) intoxicants, (6) partaking of solid food and certain liquids after noon, (7) abstention from (a) dance, song, music, shows (attendance and performance), (b) from perfumes, ornaments, etc., (8) luxurious beds. This set of eight precepts is observed by devout Buddhist lay followers on full-moon days and on other occasions.

III. The Ten Precepts: (1)-(6) = II, 1-6; (7) = II, 7 (a); (8) = II, 7 (b); (9) = II, 8; (10) abstention from acceptance of gold and silver, money, etc.

9. The other three items of the monk's fourfold pure conduct are control of the senses, purity of livelihood, and pure conduct concerning the monk's requisites.

10. Access (or "neighbourhood") concentration *(upacāra-samādhi)* is that degree of mental concentration that approaches, but not yet attains, the full concentration *(appaṇā-samādhi)* of the first absorption *(jhāna)*. It still belongs to the sensuous plane *(kāmāvacara)* of consciousness, while the *jhānas* belong to the fine-material plane *(rūpāvacara)*.

11. *Pañcupādānakkhandhā.* These five groups, which are the objects of grasping, are: (1) corporeality, (2) feeling, (3) perception, (4) mental formations, (5) consciousness.

12. Also called *sukkhavipassanā-yānika.*

13. Literally: "according to their true nature and function."

14. This method of meditation aims at "knowledge by direct experience" *(paccakkha-ñāṇa),* resulting from mindfulness directed towards one's own bodily and mental processes. It is for that reason that here express mention is made of "one's own life continuity." Having gathered the decisive direct experience from the contemplation of his own body and mind, the meditator will later extend the contemplation to the life-processes of others, by way of inference *(anumāna).* See, in the Satipaṭṭhāna Sutta, the recurrent passage: "contemplating the body, etc., externally."

15. "Noticing" *(sallakkhaṇa)* is a key term in this treatise. The corresponding verb in the Pali language is *sallakkheti (saṃ + lakh),* which can be translated adequately as well as literally by "to mark clearly." Though the use of "to mark" in the sense

of "to observe" or "to notice" is quite legitimate in English, it is somewhat unusual and unwieldy in its derivations. Hence the rendering by "noticing" was chosen. "Noticing" is identical with "bare attention," the term used in the translator's book *The Heart of Buddhist Meditation.*

16. The Sub-commentary to the Brahmajāla Sutta explains as follows: "Things in their true nature *(paramatthadhammā)* have two characteristics or marks: specific characteristics and general characteristics. The understanding of the specific characteristics is knowledge by experience *(paccakkha-ñāna),* while the understanding of the general characteristics is knowledge by inference *(anumāna-ñāna)."* The specific characteristic, for instance, of the element of motion *(vāyo-dhātu)* is its nature of supporting, its function of moving; its general characteristics are impermanence, etc.

17. The three terms printed in italics are standard categories of definition used in the Pali Commentaries and the *Visuddhi-magga.* In the case of mental phenomena, a fourth category, "proximate condition" *(padatthāna)* is added. The definition of the element of motion (or of wind) occurs, for instance, in the *Visuddhimagga* (XI. 93) and is shown in this treatise to be a fact of direct experience.

18. "Purification of mind" refers to mental concentration of either of two degrees of intensity: full concentration or access concentration (see Note 10). In both types of concentration, the mind is temporarily purified from the five mental hindrances (see Note 20), which defile the mind and obstruct concentration.

19. The "other" objects may also belong to the same series of events, for instance, the recurrent rise and fall of the abdomen.

20. The five mental hindrances *(nivarana)* which obstruct concentration, are: (1) sense-desire, (2) ill-will, (3) sloth and torpor, (4) agitation and remorse, (5) sceptical doubt. For

details, see *The Five Mental Hindrances and their Conquest,* by Nyānaponika Thera (BPS Wheel No. 26).

21. Insight reaches its culmination on attaining to the perfection of the "purification by knowledge and vision of the course of practice." See Note 41 and the *Visuddhimagga,* XXI,1.

22. This passage is translated in *The Way of Mindfulness* by Soma Thera (3rd ed., BPS, 1967), p. 104, where, for our term "access concentration," the rendering "partial absorption" is used.

23. When occurring during the practice of tranquillity meditation.

24. This is the fully absorbed concentration *(jhāna)* achieved at the attainment of the noble paths and fruitions.

25. In the Commentary to the Majjhima Nikāya No. 111, the Anupada Sutta.

26. The *Visuddhimagga* says that both terms, "knowledge by inductive insight" and "comprehension by groups," are names for the same type of insight. According to the *Paramatthamañjūsā,* its Commentary, the former term was used in Ceylon, the latter in India.

27. The ten corruptions of insight *(vipassanūpakkilesa)* are first mentioned in the *Paṭisambhidāmagga* (PTS, Vol. II, pp. 100f.) and are explained in the *Visuddhimagga* (XX.105ff.). The names and the sequence of the terms as given in this treatise differ slightly from those found in the above two sources.

28. The five grades of rapture *(pīti),* dealt with in the *Visuddhimagga* (IV.94) are: (1) minor, (2) momentarily recurring, (3) flooding, (4) elevating, (5) suffusing.

29. This passage refers to the six pairs of qualitative factors of mental activity, which, according to the Abhidhamma, are present in all moral consciousness though in different degrees of development. The first pair is tranquillity (a) of consciousness, and (b) of its concomitant mental factors. The other pairs are agility, pliancy, wieldiness, proficiency, and

uprightness, all of which have the same twofold division as stated before. These six pairs represent the formal, or structural, side of moral consciousness. For details see *Abhidhamma Studies,* by Nyānaponika Thera (2nd ed. BPS, 1985), pp.81f.

30. These six obstructions of mind are countered by the six pairs of mental factors mentioned in Note 29 and in the following sentence of the text.

31. *Non-action,* non-activity or non-busyness, refers to the receptive, but keenly watchful, attitude of noticing (or bare attention).

32. *Advertence* is the first stage of the perceptual process, as analysed in the Abhidhamma. It is the first "turning-towards" the object of perception; in other words, initial attention.

33. The supramundane paths and fruitions are: stream-entry, once-returning, non-returning, and arahantship. By attaining to the first path and fruition, that of stream-entry, final deliverance is assured at the latest after seven more rebirths.

34. "Conceptual objects of shapes" *(santhāna-paññatti).* The other two types of concepts intended here are: the concepts of individual identity derived from the *continuity* of serial phenomena *(santati-paññatti),* and collective concepts derived from the *agglomeration* of phenomena *(samūha-paññatti).*

35. "The idea of formations with their specific features": this phrase elaborates the meaning applicable here of the Pali term *nimitta,* which literally means "mark," "sign," "feature," i.e., the idea or image conceived of an object perceived.

36. "With its particular structure" *(sa-viggaha):* the distinctive *(vi)* graspable *(gaha)* form of an object.

37. *Bhay'upaṭṭhāna.* The word *bhaya* has the subjective aspect of fear and the objective aspect of fearfulness, danger. Both are included in the significance of the term in this context.

38. This refers to the knowledges described in the following (Nos. 7-11).

39. *Nirojā.* Lit. "without nutritive essence."

40. According to the *Visuddhimagga*, the "insight leading to emergence" is the culmination of insight, and is identical with the following three knowledges: equanimity about formations, desire for deliverance, and knowledge of re-observation. It is called "leading to emergence" because it emerges from the contemplation of formations (conditioned phenomena) to the supramundane path that has Nibbāna as its object.

41. The *Visuddhimagga* says (XXI.130): "The knowledge of adaptation derives its name from the fact that it adapts itself to the earlier and the later states of mind. It adapts itself to the preceding eight insight knowledges with their individual functions, and to the thirty-seven states partaking of enlightenment that follow."

42. *Gotrabhū-ñāṇa* (maturity knowledge) is, literally, the "knowledge of one who has become one of the lineage *(gotra)."* By attaining to that knowledge, one has left behind the designation and stage of an unliberated worldling and is entering the lineage and rank of the noble ones, i.e., the stream-enterer, etc. Insight has now come to full maturity, maturing into the knowledge of the supramundane paths and fruitions. Maturity knowledge occurs only as a single moment of consciousness; it does not recur, since it is immediately followed by the path consciousness of stream-entry or once-returning, etc.

43. "Path knowledge" is the knowledge connected with the four supramundane paths of stream-entry, etc. Here, in this passage, only the path of stream-entry is meant. Path knowledge, like maturity knowledge, lasts only for one moment of consciousness, being followed by the fruition knowledge result-

ing from it, which may repeat itself many times and may also be deliberately entered into by way of the "attainment of fruition" (see No. 17).

44. That means that Nibbāna has now become an object of direct experience, and is no longer a mental construct of conceptual thinking.

45. The knowledge of reviewing defilements still remaining, does not obtain at the stage of arahantship where all defilements have been eliminated. It may occur, but not necessarily so, at the lower three stages of stream-entry, etc.

46. See Note 43.

47. 'The five spiritual faculties *(indriya)* are: faith, energy, mindfulness, concentration, and wisdom. For details see *The Way of Wisdom* by Edward Conze (BPS Wheel No. 65/66).

THE VENERABLE MAHĀSI SAYĀDAW

Mahāsi Sayādaw, the Venerable U Sobhana Mahāthera, was the son of U Kan Htaw and Daw Shwe Ok of Seikkhun village, which is about seven miles to the west of Shwebo Town, a one-time capital of the founder of the last Burmese dynasty. He was born on the third waning of the month of second Waso in the year 1266 of the Burmese Era (29 July 1904). At the age of six, he began his studies at a monastic school in the same village, and at the age of twelve he was ordained a sāmaṇera (novice). On reaching the age of twenty, he was ordained a bhikkhu on the fifth waning of the month of Tazaungmon in the year 1285 of the Burmese Era (23 November 1923). He then passed the Government Pali examinations in all the three classes of Pathamange, Pathamalat and Pathamagyi in the following three successive years.

In the fourth year after his bhikkhu ordination, he proceeded to Mandalay—a former capital of Burma—where he continued his further studies in the Khinmagan Kyaung Taik under various monks of high scholastic fame. In the fifth year he went to Moulmein where he took up the work of teaching the Buddhist scriptures at a monastery known as Taung Waing Galay Taik Kyaung.

In the eighth year after his ordination, he and another monk left Moulmein equipped with the bare necessities of a bhikkhu (i.e., alms bowl, a set of three robes, etc.) and went in search of a clear and effective method in the practice of meditation. At Thatōn he met the well-known meditation instructor, the Venerable U Nārada, who is also known as "Mingun Jetawun Sayādaw the First." He then placed himself under the guidance of the Sayādaw and at once proceeded with an intensive course of meditation.

After this practical course of meditation he returned to Moulmein and continued with his original work of teaching Buddhist scriptures. He sat for the Pali Lecturership Examination held by the Government of Burma in June 1941 and succeeded in passing completely at the first attempt. He was awarded the title of Sāsanadhaja-Siri-Pavara-Dhammācariya.

In the year 1303 of the Burmese Era (1941) and in the eighteenth year of his bhikkhu ordination he returned to his native village (Seikkhun) and resided at a monastery known as Mahā-Si Kyaung because a drum (Burmese: *si)* of unusually big *(mahā)* size is housed there. He then introduced the systematic practical course of Satipaṭṭhāna meditation. Many people, bhikkhus as well as laymen, gathered round him and took up the strict practical course, and were greatly benefited by his careful instructions. They were happy because they began to understand the salient features of Satipaṭṭhāna and had also learned the proper method of continuing the practice by themselves.

In the year 1311 B.E. (1949) the then Prime Minister of Burma, U Nu, and Sir U Thwin, executive members of the Buddha Sāsanānuggaha Association, requested the Venerable Mahāsi Sayādaw to come to Rangoon and give training in meditative practice. In his twenty-sixth year of bhikkhu ordination, he therefore went to Rangoon and resided at the Thathana Yeiktha, the headquarters of the Association, where since then intensive training courses have been held up to the present day.

Over 15,000 persons have since been trained in that centre alone and altogether over 200,000 persons have been trained throughout Burma, where there are more than 100 branches for the training in the same method. This method has also spread widely in Thailand and in Sri Lanka.

Mahāsi Sayādaw was awarded the title of Aggamahāpaṇḍita in the year 1952.

He carried out the duties of the Questioner *(pucchaka)* at the Sixth Buddhist Council (Chaṭṭha Sangāyanā) held at Rangoon for two years, culminating in the year 2500 of the Buddhist Era (1956). To appreciate fully the importance of this role it may be mentioned that the Venerable Mahā-Kassapa, as Questioner, put questions at the First Council held three months after the passing away of the Buddha. Then the Venerable Upāli and the Venerable Ānanda answered the questions. At the Sixth Council, it was Tipiṭakadhara Dhammabhaṇḍāgarika Ashin Vicittasārābhivaṃsa who answered the questions put by the Venerable Mahāsi Sayādaw. The Venerable Mahāsi Sayādaw was also a member of the committee that was responsible, as the final authority, for the codification of all the texts passed at the Sixth Council.

He has written several books on meditation and the following notable works may be mentioned.

(1) *Guide to the Practice of Vipassanā Meditation* (in Burmese)—2 volumes.
(2) Burmese translation of the Mahāsatipaṭṭhāna Sutta, with notes.
(3) *Visuddhiñāṇa-kathā* (in Burmese and Pali).
(4) Burmese translation of the *Visuddhimagga*, with notes.
(5) Burmese translation of the *Visuddhimagga Mahā-ṭīkā*, with notes—4 volumes.

(6) *Paṭicca-Samuppāda* (Dependent Origination)
     —2 volumes.

A large number of his discourses, based on the Pali Suttas, have been translated into English and published by the Buddha Sāsanānuggaha Association (16 Hermitage Road, Kokkine, Rangoon, Myanmar).

Mahāsi Sayādaw passed away on 14 August 1982 following a brief illness.

Of related interest from the BPS

THE SEVEN STAGES OF PURIFICATION AND THE INSIGHT KNOWLEDGES
Mātara Sri Ñāṇārāma Mahāthera

A guide to the progressive stages of Buddhist meditation by one of Sri Lanka's most respected meditation masters.

BP 506S   Softback   82 pages

LIVING BUDDHIST MASTERS
Jack Kornfield

This valuable book brings to the reader the precise instructions of twelve great meditation masters, including Mahāsi Sayadaw, Achaan Chah, and U Ba Khin.

BP 507S   Softback   320 pages

All prices as in the latest BPS catalog
(http://www.bps.lk)

THE BUDDHIST PUBLICATION SOCIETY

The Buddhist Publication Society is an approved charity dedicated to making known the Teaching of the Buddha, which has a vital message for people of all creeds.

Founded in 1958, the BPS has published a wide variety of books and booklets covering a great range of topics. Its publications include accurate annotated translations of the Buddha's discourses, standard reference works, as well as original contemporary expositions of Buddhist thought and practice. These works present Buddhism as it truly is—a dynamic force which has influenced receptive minds for the past 2500 years and is still as relevant today as it was when it first arose.

The Hony. Secretary
BUDDHIST PUBLICATION SOCIETY
P.O. Box 61
54, Sangharaja Mawatha
Kandy • Sri Lanka

http://www.bps.lk